different streets

eileen
myles
different
streets
newer
poems

WAVE BOOKS

SEATTLE AND

NEW YORK

for Leopoldine Core

different streets

caesarean toothbrush

FOR ALICE

I left it outside
for a yuk
for those that we know
who may never come
in
but riding by they'll
know what I'm
doing. They will know
I'm okay.
It's what we want
to know about
everything. We don't
want to get sprayed
by it. More than
once it's been
suggested to me

that if I looked
more closely
I'd see that it's
normal. So I live
with weird but
familiar. To traffic
it looks okay.
My jokes are mostly
travelers' jokes
I go to unusual lengths
to get what most
people get. In my defense
I like it hard.
My cat's name is Marco
Polo. His severe profile
gazing into the
dead end
of the apartment.
Hey that's not
going out.
That end goes
out. To him I just

become invisible

for a while

& to me that's

just my life.

This is being his secretary.

Worrying about how

he'll be when

he'll be anything.

Worry about yourself,

Eileen. Stabbing

things. I just did

do it for a very

long time.

In that motion

in that soothing

motion.

2008: for emma

We have our
research to
live for. Teeshirt.
The bed not so much
made
as simply
closed.

pencil poems

So much of today
no matter what
is living in hypnotism
though I'm master
I feel it has been done to me
it seems the point
is not to decide
who's ruling
who in this tiny kingdom
of my dream
my cell jouncing yours
chest out
straight
though I am a butterfly
a buttery day in
Hawaii
referred to continually
but it was borrowed

slipped on

like

a shoe

I suppose Buddhism

is to face the

tiny dream(s)

the conviction

holds the stage

whoever's.

pencil poem #2

Is it wrong to think
you're getting excited
he pulls the window
down on the golden & brown
now I remember
when I began to speak
I began to speak
like him. I *mime*.

pencil poem #3

I stole this
it would have made
the person who manned
the list glad
this fat pencil
but I surrounded it
with need.
Vacillating
doesn't help anyone.
It's a cry for proof
Uncannily the
conditions shift
the late plane moves
everyone and even
though I doubted
now I can't
I'd like to take
the vacillating disk

and drop it in
the trash
but I imagine it turning
dying, killing me
slip in the new
1600 schedule
baggy & loose
time for a shower
I'm just going to change
my underwear not
my clothes.
I look like a pencil.
This is what I meant.

The new poems
are poems of
healing.
But first I'll
be funny.

pencil #4

A dog walks into a barber
shop.
I'm not into gender
OK says the barber
so don't think of me
as a bitch
but just one of your regular
customers
who wants to do something
a little different
I'm okay with that
said the barber.
Hot towels warm my
head, smelling of
mint. Warm lather
on my neck. Woof woof
You're a dog.
No I'm not.
And I bit him.

#5

Half asleep; generous
clatter of straws
a cup into a plastic bag.
Eyelids flutter
gulp of decent coffee
and back to nod
it's a strange gig
this body I'm riding
for 59 years.

#6 in and out

cute 50 something top
will bring you to life.
Butch bottom wants
tender master. At
the bottom of this
pencil is an eraser
something soft that takes
it away. I may have
had my "lovers"
my partners. That
was a waste. Here
I'm casting about
for my parts. Ingredients
for enjoyment. Anyone
can be beautiful
at 19 or 30. This
is life. Take a deep
look.

november 11

It's not just that
the clock
stopped or reversed
but just seemed
to change
itself
I remember
a procession
of sweet
buildings
boarded up
finding him
in a store
then kissing
in the rain
the strange pleasure
of pleasing
someone me

then my godmother
and then
someone jumping
off a building
in the rain
the surprise
and the sound
of rain
on the phone
holding it
for a while

the nervous entertainment

just when I
thought I should
break it up
the other one
licked from
across the
room. A red
echo, and a blue
one slithered
on the star
leg of an
eames type
office chair

I saw
a rainbow in

a gush today
soft green
mountain I
couldn't write
about cause
my recorder
kept checking
itself &
wouldn't work.

I'm happy
cause I don't
work. I'm like
a band that
tours people's
houses playing
when they're
not around

when Cathy
said I love
poetry I thought

well that's

cause it's

going to happen

here. It's

gonna contain

that remark. After

it enjoys

your fire. When

Cathy said wait

till you see

the morning I said

I'm excited

though it sounded

like *I*

was dead.

I don't have

a working voice

I just have

a voice that

comes out the

way it

wants apart
from me. I think
of voices
I admire & try
to use
& you
know how
your friends
shirts are.
Sometimes
it does look
good. These
jeans are
dead. They're
getting re-
placed.

Though not till
after
I finish
my novel.
Robert Walser

did huge
things in
tiny spaces.
If I say
thank you
at one
more gas
station
I'm going to start
believing oil
is god. But
it's when

I'm still
in the
landscape
the numbers flip
the land is
great

The cat is in
the bag
I leave the bag where
it is
so the cat can get
in it and dream
for a very long
time
while the rest
of my building
purrs

he slipped his head
into the bag's
handles & gently
sniffs it

well then money
well then love

seagull

The beautiful poems
of this fall
apples with dents
sitting next to a big square
of black
and burning sounds
that's rain
and trumpets
that's a car
Elliott Smith
sang high like an
angel
his little pockmarked
face and greasy
hair
cut mine like that.

the movie

He's like a train station
it's too late
to go duck hunting
at last he woke
up. Sits on blankets
with young girls
can you stand it
he does not miss
life now
in its secondary
summer
the lateness of
his first kiss

the birds

I sort of like
myself each day
as you express
your longing looking
out the window
I witness your back
I groaning and
waiting for the
grains to soak their
minutes
reading some stray
thing eight years old
you pounce: oh.
Everything does its
work. Bold or hidden?
I enthuse to under
lining   moving you
again. Bigger more

insistent desires
remind me of the
friend I must call
and what remains
of last night
accompanies
me to a
surprising wet
street. Returned
the formula & some
of the work's
done in my absence.
I *will* call you.
Like the book
your gift has arrived
inside me daily
now the underlining
to hold onto and be
heard now in the
wake of the new
knowledge. Just before
finishing I interrupt

to say. Confident
in my relationship
to some sentence
some thing. And when I
thought your sweetness
would be left
you are gone.

leaving

I saw a lightbulb
flickering
I moved towards it
and it was morning
help me birds
I stood in it
help me dog
I don't need to tell you everything
do I
in my perfect life
I like the blues
This morning solid
behind the trees
in my dream a group of
women
had one thing or two
at the supermarket

all of them (us)

were winding around the aisles

~~standing in lines~~

all my dreams were true

You said

you'd write a poem

about blue

that's what you were

dreaming

blue in a painting

blues in the sky

pale blue water

tower

reminding you of the bedroom

upstairs, it's become

your home that subtle

color that held art

so well

it's sitting there

right next to the slightly

greenish

it's windy this morning
go out and see it
don't wait till you're leaving
I love that blue.

la neige

It's like
this show will never end

was I shitting on the altars
in the nook of the zendo
in the artist colony

I couldn't help myself
I thought it was a crime
I mean I forgot

No, *my* Alcoholism

accepting inappropriate love

one of the some

like five days of rain

again & again
increasing the
distance

mouse in the backfield

it hasn't stopped
blowing to the left

I announce my

new compass

my face work

I attach my thermometer

much of
  the excitement
    is getting really
      close.   to
      describing the self

almost the
self   scary
me (the room
laughs)

but then

not. The

snow is hot.

your name

It's very hard
to hunt
from indoors
I'll say that for
you. And
text is
at best
an attenuated
warning
sound has
a range
of many desires
not just map.
I subscribe
to the grandpa
bunny bunny school
of theory
I mean genesis

to write

is a form

of accounting

& approximate

promise

in the sunny

mouth of

time. A horny

bet. Or else

hunters

lolling around the fire

what did you

get. How can

we avoid it.

This "making

a speech." Long limbed

& maybe

in July. Aren't

we lucky to have

captured each

other in this

hideous neon light.

mitten

It's beautiful. I mean
it's beautiful *here*
but the thing
is it is beautiful.
The peach sky is beautiful
and black outlines
of the branches
and the leaves
look I even
hesitate but it doesn't
matter if it all comes
at once or breaks
down slow. Catch this
honking or the rumbling
of the world. Last
night in "Different
Streets" which I didn't
bother to write I made
the point that the two places

are connected and it's great
where you are too
and boom boom rumble
all the places are connected
thus the endless
beauty. And I have been
beaten & suffered and you
have too. Whoop whoop
listen to that someone
getting arrested. Someone
caught, someone's heart
just stopped. Someone
else holding the bag.
I wrote something else
about the day holding me
and me holding you. A car
passes like a big breath.
It's what I've got: all these
things and I hand them
to you like sex in the city.
My ideal. Our endless
sound. Our connection.
Listen to *all* your voices now.

hi

FOR STEVE CAREY

You made me smell.
I didn't smell at
all before I met you
smells are pouring out of
my clothes, feet, my
socks my hair
this is gross
you've made me monstrous
and I love it
I knew a man who laughed
at himself
for being this way
stinking of love
it was what he was
a stinking factory of his love
lying there all day

going out to get a smoke
I'm the east coast version
of that
since I met you
since the era of my famous
resistance to you ended
it began like the wind
I am a window to the world
the mailman can see me
he waves; children out there playing
it's even this way when I'm out
there
except when I hold your hand
I want it; to be this exception
I've become
not a woman or a man
The heart pumps
the man is dead and it's
spring
it's a smelly season
don't you think
the earth knows

the bugs are beginning to look
around
you're throwing your mother's
old stuff out
your friends are beginning
to understand
I want to show
mine something different
the ripples I've become
I'm influence
the way language changes
and rocks heal & burn
meat stretches
your little round animal
face keeps coming around
the corner but
oh no now you're coming down
I'm looking up

idiot ho

everyone! I want
a big apple
and hey
you don't live here anymore

saw your email
I got your address

hey yellow shoes
my shirt is
yellow too

is it mad
to say I
like May
so so so
much
at this exact moment

stupid, wet

june 5

what is the nuisance
or new thing
about red angles
bars of light
in your new-named
green bank

I love you

Trumpets!

became

Just became night
in response to the enormous
history
doors swung
the fish with the human
teeth gnashed
the lighting changed subtly
in the restaurant
the handsome young man in my building was nearly
locked out
he's a terrible sleeper
and I believed him
the black man
didn't believe me
it's my house I thought
I'm not to be in this position
I liked the girl
but she didn't call

it was yesterday

today

is so subtle

I can jam tiny details

in its jaw

& it holds them

it's a strong day

that can withstand change

the weather

FOR ALAN, MONICA & FRANCES

For the most
compelling
birthday party I'd
been to in
a while
I bought three
cards.

Thinking that
I heard a wet
and sparkling
sound three pipes
spurting
water standing in the
park quite
near to the corner

I meet you on
I go past.
I don't know what
tonight will de-
liver
the teeshirt

you'll wear
an attachment
I'm proud
of not knowing
you again
like that water
I've lived here
for a while.
What do you think
I should say
in these
cards?

I'm as excited
about this moment

as I was in the

beginning

I keep seeing

women in the street

who resemble

my mother her

wide Christian

face. Is it an abomination

to put that

in a poem to

my lover

not so much to

you as with

you in it

in the same world

of the card

the train-ride into

Brooklyn

cars turning

skateboard

splash

hard the plastic

of the wrong side
hitting the
pavement. All you
see are cops

cars & their
vans prowling
like a city
full of
meth. Or whole
middle of a
country
like a split.

Every woman your
age
cute. Every woman
my age
wounded &
glisten.

smile

It's just not as much fun without a good
light and a sharp knife
I mean leaning into the peach of
it. People find the time
to get theirs sharpened or use yours.
That drip in the kitchen is like
someone I know. Today's cold
is like an affirmation of the purchase
of yesterday's new shirt. I knew the cold
would come some time but today.
I'm wearing that drip most of all.
My half-made meal and even the space
that surrounds the incredible possibility
of hunger on and on like my favorite man
Frankenstein. The drip has tones.
A relationship with the holding
bowl that is only holding water.
All these rhymes all the time. I used to

think Mark Wahlberg was family.
So was Tim but close to his death
he told me he was adopted. Every
time he smiled he thought Eileen
is a fool. Or that's what love looks
like. If I woke and my master was horrified
I would go out into the world with this
enormous hurt. And I have carried mine
for so long I now know it's nothing special.
It's just the fall and the sound of her sirens. It's the agony
of being human. Not a dog who dies maybe six
times in the lives of her masters. Everyone's phony
and made up. Everyone's a monster like me.
Now I know everyone.

the perfect faceless fish

It is a miracle
that I should speak
to delight you.
I feel like a flag
more or less
but music is my breeze
I have many friends
rest assured.
You have given me
my water
and for this I must
thank you. You have
been described
as elegant in your time
and it is long
the road to go
I am honored to accompany
you. A picture

is simply what I am
an old crease
a perfect book
you will miss me
in your sterile anticipation
of something to hang
this picture on. I come
& go. An edible saint.
But if you feast
on me you will be hungry.
I know your intelligence
carnal somehow
and I began to speak
when you began to want
me. Please don't interrupt
I cross my legs
I flood the darkened
rooms of art

for a while.
And frankly that moment
is gone.

We could only talk through
our eyes and now
that is gone. But this
is deeper than
the marrow
we don't need rods   cones
those sanskrit piles of things
I am seeing through a stain
right now
in your love
I am swimming for years.
In a sudden absence
of trouble in a deftly
handled conversation
I, a luminous fish
felt in this spectacle of impossibility
a fragrant graze upon the
world
an intermittent twitch,

whisper. If I had hands
I would touch everyone

I vanish in the green
of the background
that goes on and on
made by those who recognize
it that way
there is always something better
to do
I live in a terminal
and so do you
listen we are trying to end everything
by this enormous silence
brief
but it was the old thing
so it shall be very loud
very loutish in the squabbles we
have about right & wrong
& where the flagpole is and
do we ever
will we ever have enough
space to play the game
I am deeply knowing you
and feel you have chosen

me for this conversation
before it's cooked
before anything is prepared
anything at all
the lesser details never mind
the first exquisite choice
that brought me into being
this conversation
a fishy birth
I've had you in my pocket
it's all that I know
but a knowing that is useless
without this acknowledgment
in a many chambered room
ew
is that what you said
enormous darkly I accept it
I flow around and fold
into everything your comic
desultory contempt
which I'm beginning to see
functions as glue

for you
the prettiness for me is
the opening city
and moving through it with you
the young old fold
around your mouth
seismic
trust that
I am gold in the reconciliation
gold in the anticipation
paradise great ambiance
what's available
is not of any use to
what is me today
a stoic longing symbol of
studying peace
in outlandish quarters
your long room in the night
your whole long body
which is faceless too
to acquire your trust is of
utmost importance to me

I am foolish I talking fish
the time is here for me
to make promises to
you that is sometimes standing
in a bakery
laughing becomes a professional
wife with empty folders
and I see the muscle
embedded the one
that can't be removed
in the beloved text that is
offered
a torso sized drink to me
each time I break the surface
turn around
bubbles cascading from
the incommensurate
path of my tale, tentacle
limbs
you make me enough
so I hold a cup
gasping with laughter

in the teeshirts covered with
arcane scribbles
carry the message
awkward grins and phones to
their ears
yours are wired to everything
there is
you're an impossible telephone
I lift my head for the
last sip of your
ew
a lamb leaps over the fins
the arms I would
have we would hold
each other in
I am waiting. No difficulty
with gold. As I told
your mother I have
obtained access
to an uncontrolled intimacy
fear not
certainly I did not phrase it

like that
but I met her in
the most advanced
communication terrain
and exchanged
messages concerning our
difficulties with god
and man
I am beginning to know
I am gold a transforming
ship
the clipped end of an
utterance I was saving
for you when I saw your

swinging light
the door approach
and everything moves
  close

about mary

I feel infinity
seeing a band
of white flesh
against your dark
blue shirt
in the night
later when you turned
the ac on cause
it was hot it made it
quieter then
a little bit of fat
helps you
sleep. I thought
eating my yogurt
staged the
room for the photographer
and now I'm
in it

you have anything
crusty like your poem
abt dancing
all night in the 80s
I never danced all
night in the eighties
it was stories
& you never recorded
admit it
I'm not in that movie
Case closed.
Maybe they were richer
it worked better
Were men
or something like that.
I'm not done
w you yet playing w
your bib no apron
in the store
when you changed
your mind I thought
you had taken mine

into account.
Change it back.
Which mind was
that. A system
isn't so much closed
as sinister
no I mean conceptual
a dog gets the wrong
idea from repeated
indulgence. I don't need
to pay 45 dollars
an hour to know
that I know it. You
prefer a friendship
with her. That's not wit.
My words are big and wide
twice in the same
week. I considered it my
big mistake. You've
got to be brave
or a better word
for not knowing what's

to come. Adjusting to
that moment
or all of them. I refuse
to do any more. She wrote
it so young and she
had a funny accent
I will never
again illustrate my
widening point
with a detail
from your ex's facebook
photos. I will stop
it here by saying
I'm sorry and crossing
it all out. S has
a moustache. If I
fear I'm a failure
say no be enormous
I was/I am
if it's not for some
incredible future
everyone's & not your kids'

cause they're yours
especially if I borrow
them once in a while
as many rounds
of this as I can take
if I put more space
around each night or
day. Or just everything
minute, other things,
chairs I move the
chairs around
and make it roomier.
The words kept moving
around and not in
the terminal but in the
home. It ate
all night. I remember
you in Ireland.
I thought you had
it. Everybody had.
The amazing stories
about translators

that they speak
across
peoples all of
them. I said
I am recommending
this as the most
fun I ever
To animate the way
another saw headlights
or sound, to see a pattern
and enter their
body. I'm the galvanizing
I'm the animating
kind. I'm the monster
I shall cry till the
end of my life.

to the mountains

when I look out
at you
how absurd to think
of Diet Coke
killing me
I'm flying through
the air
and there you are
white and dangerous
who's kidding who

your house

I've walked past your childhood several
times
and friends of mine babysat
your friends. The enormous calm
this morning kernels
flowing through my clenched
fist into
an old fashioned milk bot-
tle exactly I've
constructed this time, I thought
waves, wooden ones
no, flames. As
a good middle
I climb on top
and then politely
move over. I was sexually
abused by an

entire house

every shake of the building

was my lover

me abandoning you for not noticing

me. Eating alone

for years

in my family

not putting my foot

down but not picking it

up either. Suddenly strong

in the new presumed

position. Wider than

no more private

than yes. Everyone's with

men all of

a sudden. Men made

like my time

in the morning didn't

choke the limits

of the bottle

can leave me

in satiety.
Not safety
something more
native. Listen
to me going all horny. Play
lover, play.

what's open?

is everyone
laughing at the
same thing
jay st.

borough hall

my nature is
modest

It must be hard
to have red
hair go white
you used to be
so loud & now
you're quiet

how to be brash
in the new
unreddened
space.

popsicle

after the bearded
men &
the coffee
cleaned up
pure streams
navigate your hands
our son is a puzzle
the buildings have
met; your long
legs navigate
the kitchen
sweet clatter
cluck our eggs
are done. Now everything's
heading to the
forest to feed
on me.

no california

The only time I
may've had
a kid
was at 19
and if that kid
also had a kid
at 19, then at
38 I'd be a
grandmother.
And if that
kid, next year,
also had a kid
I'd be a great grandmother.
It's late
so I want
to call
someone
in California
but I'm *there*.

snowflake

Freeze
traffic

.

my box

in terms of
design one
box is colored
orange

the one you wanted
always is and
sits in the bathroom
of anyone's
house cause
that's what
she wants
it's choosing
that wakes things
up

I wondered how
long all

that I needed and encountered

here

would come like a wave

not the shake

but the after

effects

and this box

did say

there was a way

to see this

thing

a-

lone

July called

it calculus

what is

comes in boxes

what is not

comes in waves

the dots

between

mountains
surround us
and I say
they are more
marvelous than
the sea

way overhead

I like flying over
them too
thinking
that is home
these crazy bumps
when we drive
into them
tomorrow
it won't be bam
it means up
swirling on the
edge of a
cup and if you

don't watch
me like a
hawk I won't
be scared
I want to be
loved like
a sunbeam
that is
it comes
across the room
or the ocean
you know the
way I drive
I want to lift
your fear
like a bonnet
and kiss
your living
face. Here
this is
mine. Don't
misunderstand
me.

perfect night

Youth
itself
is a little
baby animal
we're petting
his honey fur
as night
cars pass
in Missoula.
We won't leave
here or anywhere
without each
other. The
road is long
we have
our wires
trembling

I'm so there

says the

cat

glowing stick

I'm probably now and always was

a real and complete idiot

one lies on its back by the bed

glowing stick

a wand to shave my head

to call; to paste my hybridity

onto

what is it thus

a meaning of a meeting of a meeting

I say a kiss

the stripes are enormous day

and night and we like

the enormity of

fuck and love

the impossible words that leave

us on our platforms in the

sun, spinning

I want to be on a beach with you too

a beach on Mars!

there was a woman I claimed I would be dead

with if I couldn't

have her alive

and you are greater

than either in this synapse

you float in going what

the tiny stick goes orange

and then not. You can't even see

us. Cause we're everything

else. And it's ours. And I

love you in the blind spot

our changing ages.

acknowledgments

Some of these poems are transcriptions. "Call It In" was recorded on a cellphone one morning in a park in San Diego while walking my dog and I didn't have a pen. This poem was subsequently included on the Orpheus CD (Pocket Myths #3).

The set I vaguely think of as "the LA/Driving poems" (*Snowflake*, pages 26–40) were dictated onto a small digital recorder while I drove from San Diego to Los Angeles at twilight then night. These poems originally appeared on *Intervalles 4/5: Interdisciplinary Transcriptions*. I'd like to thank their respective editors (Andrea Lawlor and EE Miller) and Andy Fitch and Jon Cotner for making a home for these (to me) new-seeming poems which I later discovered were not new at all but merely older than 'writing.' In response to these (I think) I wrote a set of 'pencil poems' which were in praise of the fine fat pencil I was using, stolen from the mailing list in the lobby of INTAR, NYC. I apologize but damn what a good pencil. I'd like to thank Charles Alexander of Chax Press, Tucson, AZ for publishing *Pencil Poems* in a gorgeous small 'chapbook.'

And I'd like to thank the great friends and editors who published many of the other poems which appear in this book: *Massachusetts Review, Past Simple, Coconut, Washington Square, Come Here!, Tin House, Bombay Gin, phati'tude, The Nation, HOW, The Best American Poetry 2010, Brooklyn Rail, jubilat, Kadar Koli, Vanitas Magazine, Vice, Serpentine Gallery Poetry Marathon, Eleven More Women Poets in the 21st Century, Fact-Simile, Conversations at a Wartime Café, Bird Fly Good, VLAK, Ploughshares, West 10th, Bone Bouquet.* If I've forgotten any other publications just know it was because of the wildness of the time—moving etc. and just know I'm totally grateful for your support of my work. I'd like to thank the MacDowell Colony and the Poetry Society of America for the Shelley Award and my friends in LA—Cathy de la Cruz, Mark So and Maggie Nelson and Harry Dodge—and at the UMT, Missoula, specifically Brian Blanchfield, Katie Kane, Prageeta Sharma, Casey and Karin Schalm. And Mary Jane Nealon. You all made a beautiful place real for me. Across the board for this book and everything it is, I love you, Leopoldine Core.

SNOWFLAKE

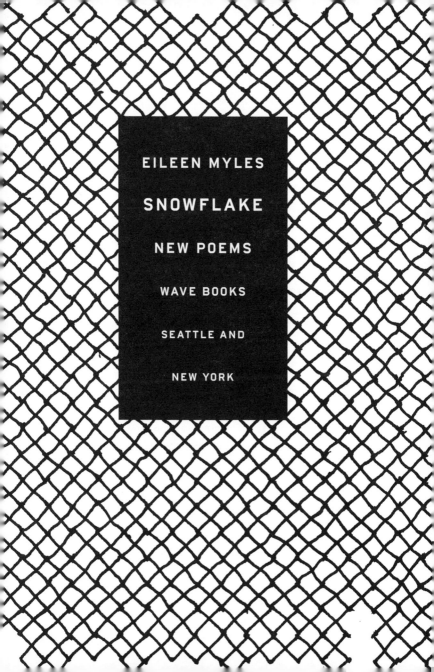

EILEEN MYLES

SNOWFLAKE

NEW POEMS

WAVE BOOKS

SEATTLE AND

NEW YORK

PUBLISHED BY WAVE BOOKS

WWW.WAVEPOETRY.COM

COPYRIGHT © 2012 BY EILEEN MYLES

WAVE BOOKS TITLES ARE DISTRIBUTED TO THE TRADE BY

CONSORTIUM BOOK SALES AND DISTRIBUTION

PHONE: 800-283-3572 / SAN 631-760X

THIS TITLE IS AVAILABLE IN LIMITED EDITION HARDCOVER

DIRECTLY FROM THE PUBLISHER

LIBRARY OF CONGRESS CATALOGING-IN-PUBLICATION DATA

MYLES, EILEEN.

SNOWFLAKE : NEW POEMS / EILEEN MYLES. — 1ST ED.

P. CM.

ISBN 978-1-933517-58-2 (ALK. PAPER)

I. TITLE.

PS3563.Y498S65 2012

811'.54—DC23

2011030700

COVER LETTERING BY XYLOR JANE

DESIGNED AND COMPOSED BY QUEMADURA

PRINTED IN THE UNITED STATES OF AMERICA

9 8 7 6 5 4 3

FIRST EDITION

WAVE BOOKS 030

SNOWFLAKE

TRANSITIONS

for Rocco

sometimes
I'm driving
and I pressed
the button
to see who
called &
suddenly I'm
taking pictures.
Big dark
ones. He says
it's not about
where you sit
to make a
film
but I wasn't
taking a

picture
I was driving
it's black &

there's all
these lights
I'm strong
it's night
& I've

driven very
far

I keep hearing
the music
of the weekend
he says
it's not about
whether she & I
resume
it's how it goes

on
with me.

In my car
so long ago
I loved someone
who read me a poem
on the phone
about the car
of the day

you mean the
one I'm driving

and the fact that
she left it
on the phone
and that was new

she said I was overreacting

and that was too much

and we sent our messages

in light

and ack she hated

trees

I thought she's so

young cause

I like nature

now and her trunk

wrapped around

me one day

he licks my

arm my boy

& driving home I thought

if he dies

I will see his paw

in the sky

I am seeing it now

and she's always

home

going hwuh

and she said

I love our little
meeting I said

little

don't denigrate
my need to support

my need to say
that you *can*

I'm glad I'm
home   it's wide
out there
we spoke about scaf-
folding
him fitting the
frame to the
eye
she's grown
I wanted to say
we laughed about

tang
and later on the
toilet
thought
about tango
and joan
L Tango Larkin
what's not technology
what's not seeing
an arm to say
I hold the
line   I hold
the day
I watch the snowflake
melting

DAY

She perceives
light
as a paint by
number
leaping into
a dark two
a puddle
to the hump
of her breathing
her sharing
the air
I join in
it's everywhere
with her
her abdomen
bobbing
as she stands
looking at

the fence,
ground
the splay
of the light
her wonderful
ass sits
down.
Earlier
I ascribed
her feeling
to joy
number one
or else
three:
birds, 8
her pink tongue
four
darker underneath
seven
the birds
sounding like

9
and a brown
tree over
there
living
or dying
in the
blue air

NO EXCUSE

The crows
were never here

I don't remember them
and you could
put your hand in the water
& hit a fish or two

now you gotta
go look.

She was the first one from
India to outer space.

I don't remember
those trees
and I don't remember
it being so hot

but winter used to be
really cold
You remember that.
I know to hold back
tends to keep the thing
going but I don't

I like it kind of square
all there.

We played the reading
at Gallery 6
maybe it was his
description of it.
We read it
in class

some things get saved.
I like to return.

I like the farmer
who studied science
came home

and made it work
He was Japanese.
He stabbed himself right
in the chest. Like
Elliott, not Kurt.

The two kinds
of death are different.

Of all the songs
you ever wrote
you wrote some

guy in the airport
reading about farming
big thick thighs
and he looked like a businessman
and that's what farmers
look like today.

He was trying to get better. To improve
his lot

this immense restlessness on the
plane

      remembering Rae
thought the birds had changed

and something else

and Peter said the fish
were practically everywhere
and now they're not.

I don't know myself
and that's a sin.

OBSERVANCE

the thing

about Los Angeles

the way

the cars

pile up

when you

get close

you'd think

they had

something

really good

in there

~~NO RAIN~~

And then
I heard
the sound
of rain
that's the
air conditioning
but what
makes
me
want
the rain
in here.
That's you
says
Chris
being con-
nected
but no

I hoped
the darkness
meant
something.
I put
the heat
on before
I left
so I
could
come
in to
something
warm
not cold
bereft.
But it
wasn't that.
Just
grey cold
drunken
grey

a day
full of
sticks and
plans and
flowers
for you.
I want
to wrap
them
in bamboo
or clay
I want
to hang
them on your
door
opening
the marvelous
concrete
truths
of what
you're doing
now with

your hands
and ideas
I have
a secret
for you
the rain
is falling
through
a screen
I see
many of
us
I hear
a roar
what's that
I asked
Chris.
That's the
future
he said.
It's
true

WRITING

I was looking
at the chandelier
do you
feel that
way she
asked
I was driving
through
Los Angeles
getting
some help
I didn't
know
Pema Chödrön
was a girl
People
sounded
nuts

She had a
sign

I'm hungry
I'm homeless
with a really
pretty sun

She hadn't
asked
for anything
but I gave
her five
and that
felt great
I thought
women are
a bunch
of idiots
but that's
what I

am are U
one

I don't count
on what
I am
she
said

and that
chandelier
is more
light

than
anyone
else

SNOWFLAKE

There's no female
in my position

There's no man

wow
there's a raccoon
on the tail
of the plane
and there's
no one

seeing that now
but me

and there's no one close
enough right
in here

to see the
further
drawing
stripes or buildings
the bricks
of the world
I wonder
what I'll say about Sadie
and I wonder
if they are still
living in that
state
and if they hate
me for moving
her furniture
out and putting
it in storage

I walked past that restaurant
where I was so mad
I could have broke
the glass

I'm the only one in the mood to remember
this me living

who threw
a snowball
against the
glass
and scared
me in my seat
so hot
with rage
why am I dry
freezing
I want to go
home

I saw a rose
in the heart
of the
year two thousand one
everything
turning

rose
dog head
a wheel of
love
but I was so mad

I locked it
up and took
the key and lived
for that moment
snowflake
I wasn't there
not even me
when she put
in the key
and it wouldn't
turn

#1 (WITH MUSIC)

This is the emerging
possibility of writing
this way
down a thimble of
a street with a cake of a
view
bushy imported trees
& the pop music given
to me by some young
person in fact
the one person I know

#2

Those cars
enter like
a spider drizzle

look at me
sun drenched black

using my foot instead of my toes for a change
I count this road
I read that chain where you sit down
is easier fat than
fast food
what do you know red trucks with their hiccup
front
grant wood roads
I know you're not a microphone

I know you're god
I know what catches me & stops me all the time

and fills the rest
and fills the bill
and swells
and comes down

#3 (PEACH . . .)

My need to meet the new technology head on

Tommy's restaurant

San Clemente State Park

a red car zipping past a lump of cheese

wall they built for some purpose
to look like the houses they built
overhead

peach!
peach!
peach!

#4 PALM TREE

I use my nail to write
the pressure of my hand

I mark time by palm trees that *are*
and live next to one that
that was

a tall brown dead stick
poking the sky that I use as a marker
to say turn here

right now

#5 DRIVING

Driving
wiving with the
land

#6 (EILEEN . . .)

that ride took at least an hour
longer than it usually does

big brown clown mountains
to my left the last part of the trip
here is wide open sky
and I forgot this
and I forgot that
and in my freedom
I forget why I leave
Eileen,
I leave
my name.

#7 DARK WATER

big parkways so disturbing to me
some cars seem to erupt from the
the tar itself
they seem to pull
themselves up
from below the surface of the land
though I don't think land. I mean something
    flat, something
black
almost like a water that we're on
though a dark water that
holds us.

#8 CAR CAMERA

my bullet regular
my two-fisted slim little
gun of a man

now to touch a button
and turn the entire outside of my
car into a camera
so that everything that's going
on out there could be coming in
could be held and recorded
cause I don't want to point the camera

I want it to be as open as I am

what's moving *be* the thing
that holds it all
I think that dot is me

ferris wheel, bridge, trusty grey & pink scarves
of secondary color decorating
the light blue but as we know
darkening sky.

#9 DESTROYING US

I don't mean to romanticize
this thing that's destroying
us all
I would happily drive
more than two hours
no
I would drive . . .

romanticize this thing
that's destroying us
I would drive
a couple of hours
for friendship.

#10 BALL

Is there anything about oil we don't
know already
like we're driving on our own limited past
something that's ancient like the history of
this ball we're driving these cars on
the fluid of everything and everybody
that ever was here
we're draining that
to just get around

and it's nice that
I could feel around in
the dark to say
these things
to touch a button
to make it light
and then
go out

#11 THE LINES

We're both here
in the dark and I can't
feel you

I don't know what
you're saying

just stay in your
lines

#12 MAN'S BEAUTY

we go this way and
you go that

things are a lot better
for us now

a man's beauty
remains the one thing
you are absolutely
not allowed to
discuss

it's not a subject
he'll tell you
so his beauty winds
up being like that of god

you can be yammering
outside of the castle
god's not going to come out
just so you can see what the

oh shut up

ANDREA VILLA

a building says
I'm gorgeous inside

CALL IT IN

I am a bad
place

without pen
and paper
the flowers fall
squiggly trees
San Diego morning
table top wet
with sprinkler's
grief
and the birds screaming

screaming again

I am a bad
place

There's another!

a falling flower
and a landing bird

on a tree
it's so cozy

how shade
makes borders
a dark park

I walk between
dark and light
nothing new:

follow my friend

I am a bad
place without
paper and pen

Observe
the contagion, the contention

the scream of bird
behind the invisible
bench

and another flower
falls

I am a bad place

from whence
to when

a tiny shadow
of that dark
thought

a flower fall

I like the solitude
of morning

hand on a warm
face

a close kind of
Love

of humans

hiding in the
shade

young men in the dark
of their day

if I compose
on a road

where the sky is blue
and the planes
come wombling

through

in the sky
tonight
completely dark
and alone
hurtling toward

you,
my home

if I can compose
in the air
in the dark

my place is a bad
place
without
pencil and pen

my voice
is thin
and cutting
through.

ROCK ON

I do a lot of
wrong reading
stretching a meaning (my name)
into a world
view. If
it calls Ei

leen
I look up
you don't know
how much
daily
hearing I do
when everyone's
lazy (I lean)
I get
erect

I blame
you for
not finding
me — loving

me ever,
but I am balanced
by the
abysmal
cradle
of sound. You
say I'm
tired.
I know.

QUESTIONS

I may

not have

the time

for all

of this

but (A) I

enjoy the

slap of

my flipflops

on the stair

& though my

name is

not Roxanne

I remember

when I

would've liked

that like

a girl playing

witch in

her yard

with jars

& spider

webs & the

world was

misty. (A)

almost took

it all.

Even if I'm

not Roxanne

I know

you liked

my voice

in the

dark &

I did too

(B) Rabbits

like to be

up and around

at twilight

& dusk ex-

actly when

I get

scared

Did stripes

come from

any place

else in nature

but a changing

sky & a

sad parent

fills a

room & before

a child can

think she

feels it

too.   (C) The

Tree. There

was a moment

of light

before I

got in the

car. The

tree was

that green

that holds

up the

procession

of this.

It is the

world.

(D) And now

I will drive

home. I

looked at

a lamppost

just for

a sec.

Could Eileen

ever be

Roxanne?

No.

LIKE

drinking that much

Diet Coke on the plane
to prove
I am a man
young guy down
there with
a beard looking
like a goat
and the white construction
of Oakland
huge
they went round and round
9 times
they dropped the pebbles
where they
went
this is poetry

the thousand-eyed
fly
examining the
kids
cause you know
we are equal
in the complexity
of our gaze
my face's shuttered
here's the argument
don't ask don't tell
is okay but if you con-
vinced
the army you're straight
that's wrong, right

you were lying
to me

the night's a little devil
I hold in my hand

petting holding
his head
learning his
loves. Liking
him. Digging his heat.

TO WEAVE

muzzle lowering
muzzle gleam

walk me home

one million
leaves
yellow &
brown
coming down
the drive
the breeze
opens
sweet

what were
those lies

openness
a picture
I took
to show
the world
your open
mouth
my delight
in it

as if
this saga
were
complete

it tears
above to convey
their dreams
the airport's
not far
away

who has
a rooster
who has
a shirt

who held
your pussy
for all
to see
and you came

stadiums cheer
the plane slips
the news

who would
you be now
sweetness
full of appetite
and your
walk

and I
teeny column
watch their
shirts cross
the land

and kick
and who
is she

no one
notices
you look like
one
stitched on
a hill
permanent sound
no birds
his hands slipping
in

slap her
around
& that's for
appetite
here's lunch
here's for
your handsomeness
inside
out

the rooster
crows
in the wind
I meant
it gleaming
like a sound
that's gone

a crying
ghost: *you*

& there
you go
an actual
song

the cartoons
were drawn
to pleasure
kings and
their delivery
was
guaranteed
by workers
I should
know
prepared to
revolt
because one
had a
dream a
picture he

sent me
for you
to undo

while you're
dancing on
my shield
while your
head's
thrown
back
and I grunt
an army
of lick

the flowers
froze and
your four
legs waiting
close. I wanted
to say

you are
just like
the birds
on this
day my
shield.

Forever

TRANSPORTATION

I bought a bigger
pinker dick
for you
but then I
didn't
call. It seemed necessary
you're tall
& I miss you all
the time.

I love missing
I guess
it's mostly
that. You pulled
yourself up
like a big cat
but shorn

Hate to see
you that way
so I'll just
stick
it in
the ground

I imagine you flying
around
like ancient art
all gold
don't be scared
when I call
I'll be new

I want to lie
with you
on mounds of sand
and the power of the
sun

I'm missing my boat
by the way
& all of the sudden
the voice
stops

KILLER'S CRY

Now the

cat

won't sleep

with me

& I can't

water the

plants

this causes

an enormous

yawn &

tears

come

to my eyes

the heating's

tapping

down

I wonder

if he

knows this
or that
word in
French
I hope
I wake
up. She
will only
give me
bad news
& he & I
will go
to Mexico
because
this is
my life. I
am filled
w good
things despite
her bad
news
I'm sure

she doesn't
view me
badly
That is
her job.
It's
mine to
look
for the simplest
& easiest
words w
no apparent
edge
everywhere
it's too
warm
why should
I be
difficult.
Something
bit my
cat's

neck
there's a
pout of
skin
a cut
sitting
there. Prob-
ably
a coyote
That's
why he
won't
sleep w
me. They
will all
look
sad when
I bring
him in
because
my dog
just died.

Tonight
I looked
at her
pawprint
in plaster
& it looked
like anyone's.
Where are
her long
nails.
In the
box, ashes
now. Her
name embossed
on a
plaque. It
embarrasses
me her
death where
even her
dying
was wonderful

refusing
dog food
only
steak then
we carried
her into
the
room.

phone isn't
the same string
from person to
person now
that we carry
them and
have no homes

MORE OIL

he was dead
and not a particular
rabbit
his legs crossed
like he was asleep
and I hate us
I hate our roads
his little inconsequential
ass
I think of
his nobody
running
we don't sleep
we get stuck
or burned
we are not
the kindest
of mammals

with our fucking
tar & our bombs

he painted his
driveway blue
& kept us
out
I thought: look
what you did
and she
was sleeping
in my space
no parked

is it less right
to be obsessed
with friendly
fire &
Tillman's
lying there
a lamb
are you

sure they didn't
shoot him
cause he was famous
going over the
hill for a
pass
catch this
big guy
sometimes
I don't run
I just pull over
listening to the fossil
fuel churning
in my guts
I'm leaving
this city for the
dirtier one
with more traffic
I don't belong
here either
you make me so sad
I'll stay

I'll tell you what
makes me sad
sun on grass
a beautiful
day
farting in my
car
or watching
a palm
tree do
its galloping
sigh
a bird clucks
and another
box parks

D.H.

Politically speaking

look at this

a word at a time

on my knee

looking forward to a picnic

with my friends

in the afternoon

in their car

but no the climate is such

that I never

arrive

stayed on the stair

master

one more time

I'm depressed

all my life

enraged the man behind

me as we plow

into the brite grey light

it's evening here

bright as a flea

as I enter the history

of intellectuals

who escaped *that*

to land in

this eternal

sun

burning what's left

of the earth

never meeting

anyone

CUTE

I feel like
another
Paul McCartney
story
a face is
like a sheet
made
of cream
on a pile
of bones
a pile of brown
rocks lying on
its bed

you think
I feel sad
no I hear
birds the cheers

of them
hammering
teasing the night
a cat cleans
her leg with
her mouth
a dog lies
still I'm
like that dog
cept

I'm writing
so I guess
I'm licking
too. Here,
here,

COMPUTER

I'm not even a boat

I'm where a boat

crashed.

I put my impossible

body in your hands

is this a pen

TO MY CLASS

I'm trying
to figure
out what
kind of fucked
up flower
a reflection
is
when everything
dances
in a bowl
of aluminum
day's on
no extra
light
just the color
scheme
of the gym
& thinking

about that
the tile is that
exact
shade which
is not quite
white
they chose
it and it's
why the
feeling is not
exact

I've got
to lie
down
on the mat
to see
the frond
peeping
through
the
window

sitting up there's
too much
a bending plant
a grille
the whole
life of
the gym
not the tiny
crop

like sitting in a
Muslim
restaurant
and the cow
peeps in
like that

I'm trying to
sort
out a
few things
at this

exact

moment

in my life

something

more

marvelous

than a category

the body

place is

a thinking

place

a surprise

here

a day isn't

a bookshelf

unless it's

the endless

process

of

pulling one

down

and hours or

years
later
putting it back
up for
some other reason
among its
new friends
I don't really
need
glasses
to write
but I squint
and gradually
that grows
unfamiliar

GIRLFRIEND

for Leopoldine

a ball of light
comes up
a street
meets a park,
enters.
A translucent
statue
stands inside
one that holds
the day &
explains
love to the world
even in the
dark
the roar-
ing sun

embraces the
girl
inhabits
and entrances
her. It's
the way
you know me,
I know you.
The ball
streams past
but leaves her
light
shovels its
glory everywhere
jars & cars
out paces
the stars
the world
is flooded
with
you. That
good.

UNLIKELY

Rosie
doesn't know
it's Saturday
& Flora had
an egg on a pile
of rice that
looked like
a breast

Eileen I'm
going to get
out of here &
I wish you
would too. I
know that guy
had a killer vibe
the dept. of Agriculture
says don't inspect.

children in Iowa
in 1939
were taught
to stutter
for a test.
It's warm on my
shoulders
and on my
back he hasn't
killed me yet
the baby in Queens
was taken away
his vegan parents
were starving
him

in the time
of a child
running for a ball
I know she'll never
get home
and he waits

MY MONSTER

dry cleaners
never
have to
worry
about their
sign

the worse
it gets
the cleaner
people think
their
clothes
will be

do you
see
my choice

sometimes
you have to
slow down

or speed
up to
fart. The
revolution
is still

occurring
in the
body
I want
to go
home is
what you
say out
the window

just when
I had

nothing
to say
I heard
his blah blah
blah
and I thought
well I'll
say something
else

I want
to be
in it

you might

think
I'm ignoring
you but
that's
what's
happening

I'm in you
blah blah
blah

it's *hot*

she might
see them
as pimples
on his
ass but
he sees them
as allergic
jewels

at night
in Iceland
Haraldur
goes out
to gather
a box of
darkness

they have
more time
if you think
of it

that's why
Kristin
emails me
more when
I'm
here — What's
between
us is
countries

which is
nothing
now.

I say love
blah blah

blah

I say
love

EILEEN

yes Ernie
why can you
have junk
food & I
cannot. Why can
you have a
giant plate
of pasta
and I can
no longer have
my crunchy
treats Why
am I served
up a cold
fish plate.
you're not
so thin
Eileen
I know.

HOWLAND

Stephen was a servant
that wind out there
says more

aporia
my speech is disturbing
the one million tourists
on the street today
Kenny prior to your move
to Charles River Park
you lived in Somerville
is that correct to say
Debbie said I had a knot
in my neck
Language is not greedy
as she rubbed it
Ryan's play became
illuminated

Ryan lives in Dorchester
now is that true.
Yes it is
I wonder if this
would be better without
sound. Stephen
Howland had no sea legs
fell off the boat
fortunately a halyard
was lowered and
he was raised to safety.
I read this on the
couch. At which
point do you think
his name
was attached to this
street. When they only
lived here a number
of months. Ask
Kenny.
My desire to go to the beach
has been curtailed

and you're on your vacation
the word halyard
is in my vocabulary
I am nearly broke
because of my recent
interest in sailing
my time in a boat
with Abby Swan
the name of my street
in the town
I grew up
not Provincetown
the meaning of this
name belonging to a king
hither hills another
story and
your outfit in
John's show
Dorothy Bradford
threw herself
right
off the boat.

AD

Donna Binder sent me
a jpg called ernieandnika
It's all stripes. I mean
no dog no cat just a
horizontal television Agnes Martin
of red pale blue & black
nice cause ernie's
nestled now at the back
of my spine. Construction
outside and trees
waving. Guess I
should be writing like that
not this sorry report
enjoying the pause
of nothing
being what it should
love is

SUNDAY

that was the most corrupt sit ever
looking at my watch seven minutes before
and then every few minutes
returning to the string from the top of my head
heaven
dangling there
peeking through the woods
one patch of bright blue white
finally the beeping came
I'm free to stagger around find the cat
black curled on the couch. He's been out all night
and naturally I'm concerned
20 hours out
I pat him as deep animal sounds of satisfaction
come up from his insides
I warm his joints with my hand
this is the most important thing in the world
I say aloud to everything
call me your chief fool
and I'm done

THE IMPORTANCE OF BEING ICELAND

It seems the color is constant on the sun.
Storms every few hours
and the storms are bright.
it even gets translated
here. On the beach
I'm remembering
yesterday's
paper
described a snap
and those colors come down to us
once in a while
through something like a wind sock

when I lived in San Diego
everyone was gay
in my neighborhood
it was all about selling
they came to our door and offered

us a wind sock
the waves are rolling and the sun comes out
it said I am gay too

soon those people were
gone they called them
flippers gay flippers

gone their
rainbow socks
it's a snap the colors
come rushing down the tunnel
straight to here
not where I sit but in
Iceland some time

Glenn told me about a woman
who waited her whole
life to watch the aurora borealis
she was *here*
it didn't happen
scientists now understand the nature

of the particles rustling
through the sock
the snap occurs first
the color comes later

If I sold my house
in San Diego sooner
I'd be rich

The woman wasn't standing
there to watch the sky change color
I mean it would've
been nice

a dish of light forms
an enormous pancake
called day across
the sea
and some lights
o'er the front of my legs
like a cartoon
I draw.

I am trying *to concentrate*
on *the bull*

not the language of selling

like it said in the paper

Am I the bull?

CHOKE

Of all the ways of forgetting
not turning the pilot on is not
                    the worst

The house is intact
you are floating
in time
buckets of it streaming through
              the windows

youth turned it up I think
or on & fell asleep

Remembering to do.
You are too intact
the dappled sunlight on the lawn
or pots of darkness
like salt instead of depths

Still once I turned it up
the popping commenced
like applause for the present
tense
the site of my sway

Larry's new car is wide & safe
a woman's voice conducts
us left & right
she's crazy he laughs
again & again

my shrink said buy it now
about the car

I told him about my phenomenal streak
of winning & when the stakes
rose I began to bid low &
not at all
I could have won; you choked
he said.

Woof. To not choke
is I suppose to experience
to hold it in & go forth
though you need the heat

The sun had not done more
suddenly for a while

it's like we took off our skin
and said it is hot.
It's like we sold our skin
& said where did everyone go?

when the weather's too hot for comfort
& we can't have ice-cream cones
it ain't no sin
to take off your skin
& dance around in your bones

EILEEN MYLES is the author of more than
twenty books of poetry, fiction, nonfiction, plays,
and libretti, including *Inferno (A Poet's Novel)*,
The Importance of Being Iceland (for which she
received a Warhol Creative Capital Art Writers
Grant), and *Sorry, Tree*. A former director of
St. Mark's Poetry Project, Myles campaigned as an
openly female write-in candidate for president of
the United States in 1992. She received the Poetry
Society of America's Shelley Memorial
Award in 2010. She lives in New York.